Spelling
Activity Book

for ages 6-7

This CGP book is bursting with fun activities
to build up children's skills and confidence.

It's ideal for extra practice to reinforce
their learning in primary school. Enjoy!

Published by CGP

Editors:
Keith Blackhall, Andy Cashmore, Rachel Craig-McFeely,
Katya Parkes, Jack Tooth

With thanks to Emma Crighton and Juliette Green for the proofreading.

With thanks to Lottie Edwards for the copyright research.

ISBN: 978 1 78908 626 3

Printed by Elanders Ltd, Newcastle upon Tyne.
Cover and graphics used throughout the book © www.edu-clips.com
Cover design concept by emc design ltd.

Text, design, layout and original illustrations © Coordination Group Publications Ltd. (CGP) 2020
All rights reserved.

Photocopying this book is not permitted, even if you have a CLA licence.
Extra copies are available from CGP with next day delivery • 0800 1712 712 • www.cgpbooks.co.uk

Contents

Words ending in y	2
Short vowel sounds	4
or and ur	6
Soft c	8
Soft g	10
Silent k, g and w	12
Puzzle: Wild West round-up	14
Words ending in le, el, al and il	16
Words ending in tion and sion	18
Adding ing and ed	20
Adding er, est and y	22
More suffixes	24
Adding s and es	26
Tricky words	28
Answers	30

Words ending in y

How It Works

Words that end in the **long i** sound are often spelt with a y.   spy

Words that end in the **long e** sound can be spelt with a y or with an ey.   lorry   key

Now Try These

1. The words below are all missing **y** or **ey**. If the word is missing **y**, colour the car blue. If the word is missing **ey**, colour the car red.

berr__   rel__   bab__

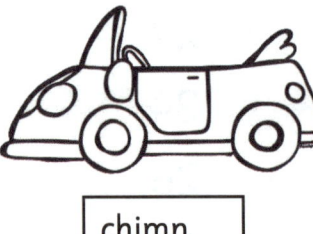  

chimn__   sh__   troll__

2. Tick the sentences below where the word in bold is spelt correctly.

The train went through the **valley**. ☐

The **jelley** wobbled on the plate. ☐

I saw hot-air balloons in the **sky**. ☐

Anna rode to school on a **donky**. ☐

3. Circle the word in each sentence with the right spelling of the **long e** sound.

The children were **happy / happey** that the bus was on time.

The sweet cost one **penny / penney**.

Henry's **hocky / hockey** stick broke.

Our dad drove us to the **party / partey**.

4. Unscramble the letters in bold to make words ending in the **long i** sound.

We'll ride our bikes if the weather is **yrd**. ➡ ....

Mark will **rfy** the eggs for breakfast. ➡ ....

Faye wanted to **alpyp** for a new job. ➡ ....

I will **ryple** to the letter from Grandma. ➡ ....

An Extra Challenge

Holly, Max and Preena have each thought of a word ending in **y** or **ey**. Can you use their clues to work out the words?

My word starts with j. It has the **long e** sound. It means a trip from one place to another.

My word starts with f. It has the **long i** sound. It is what planes do to move through the air.

My word starts with f. It has the **long e** sound. It is a type of boat that is much bigger than mine.

How was your trip through these pages? Tick a box.

Short vowel sounds

How It Works

The **short o** sound is usually written o, but after **w** or **qu** it's written a.

fr**o**g   w**a**nt   qu**a**lity

The **short u** sound can be written u, but sometimes it's written o.

m**u**d   **o**ther

Now Try These

1. Draw lines to join each word to the missing letter.

 squ__d

 sw__mp

 w__nd

 st__p

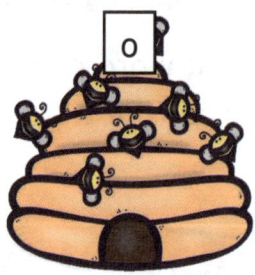 o

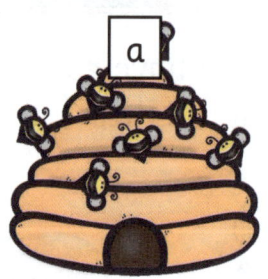 a

2. Circle the words that are spelt incorrectly. Can you rewrite them on the lines without any mistakes?

huney   cover

love

come

muther

....

....

3. Can you use all the letters on each bush to write a word with the **short u** sound?

_ _ _ _   _ _ _ _ _   _ _ _ _ _   _ _ _ _ _ _

4. Fill in the gaps with **qua** or **wa** to make words with the **short o** sound.

Fran likes to ....tch the birds in her garden.

Jake often s............bbles with his brother.

The duck ....ddled across the grass.

Lin s............shed the berry under her foot.

An Extra Challenge

Greg the Gardener has written about his day at work, but he has made some mistakes. How many can you spot? Can you correct them?

Each munth, I water Abi's garden. She has a large quontity of flowers so there are lots of bees and wosps! I have to squot down to reach a few of her plants. There's also a hedgehog who has had anuther baby.

Are these short vowel sounds growing on you? Tick a box.

or and ur

How It Works

When the **or** sound comes before **l** or **ll**, it can be written **a**.   also   call

The **or** sound is usually written **ar** when it comes after **w**.   w**ar**t

When the **ur** sound comes after **w**, it can be written **or**.   w**or**thy

     Be careful — it's easy to mix up these spellings and the sounds they make.

Now Try These

1. Can you circle the word with the **or** sound that's spelt wrong in each sentence?

I arlways talk to my coach after a game .   A swalm of bees came towards the pitch .   There were lots of balls in the sports horl .

2. Unscramble the letters in bold to make a word with the **ur** sound.

I had a **orwd** with the players.      ....

We were the **twosr** team.   ....

They **wrosihp** in a church.   ....

3. The words below are missing the **or** sound or the **ur** sound. Can you rewrite them in the box with the right spelling of the missing sound?

homew__k

w__mth

w__se

w__ld

w__drobe

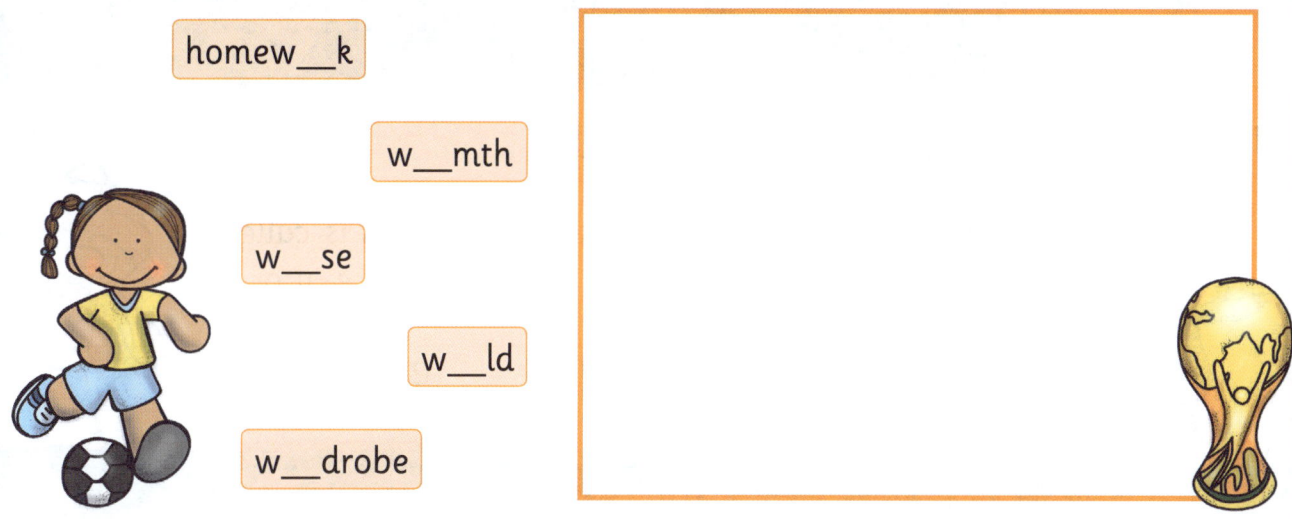

4. Circle the word in each sentence with the right spelling of the **or** sound.

Hannah went to the match with **arl / all** of her friends.

We got a **reward / reword** for working really hard.

Steven's team **almost / orlmost** won the competition.

The park **worden / warden** told us to get off the grass.

An Extra Challenge

Using words that contain the **or** or **ur** sound, can you describe something that is happening in the picture below? Write down as many sentences as you can.

Did you manage to tackle these questions? Give a box a tick.

Soft c

How It Works

The **s** sound is usually just written **s**.   silly

Sometimes the **s** sound is written **c**. This is called a **soft c**. You'll often find a **soft c** before e, y or i.

space   icy   ex**c**iting

Now Try These

1. Can you use all the letters on each igloo to write a word with a **soft c**?

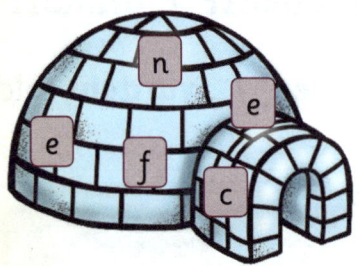

___ ___ ___ ___ ___   ___ ___ ___ ___ ___

___ ___ ___ ___ ___

2. Complete each sentence with the right spelling from the boxes.

cy   ce   ci

The sledge ra_____ was really fun.

Gemma went to the fan_____ dress party.

The walrus de_____ded to go for a swim.

3. Circle the word in bold in each sentence that has the right spelling.

   It has not snowed **sinse** / **since** last winter.

   The puppy ran at a fast **pace** / **pase** .

   Keira read the **signs** / **cigns** carefully.

   Arjun heard a **voice** / **voise** in the forest.

4. Tick the phrases below that are spelt correctly. Can you rewrite the other phrases in the box without any mistakes?

   a nice polar bear ☐   a helpful resipe ☐

   outcide the bank ☐   the singing reindeer ☐

An Extra Challenge

Fill in the gaps in these words that contain the **s** sound. Then find the words in the wordsearch. Use the pictures to help you.

fr _ _ t 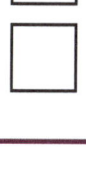   m _ _ e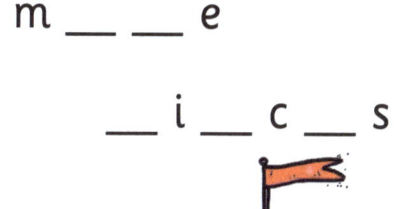

```
N J F R O S T
L U E W D R O
A I U K P H A
R C I R C U S
W Y P F L E D
C M G H O X E
M I C E B V H
```

j _ i _ y    _ i _ c _ s

Did you keep your cool on these pages? Tick a box.   ☐   ☐    ☐

Soft g

How It Works

The **j** sound is usually written j. Sometimes the **j** sound can be written g, ge or dge. This is called a **soft g**.

jump   magic   age   fudge

ge and dge are normally used when the **soft g** is at the end of the word.

Now Try These

1. Draw lines to join each word to the missing letter.

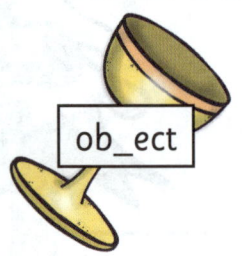
ob_ect

_oke

_iant

j

g

_entle

_ewel

en_ine

2. Circle the words where the **j** sound is spelt wrong. Can you rewrite them on the lines without any mistakes?

nudge   ege   chandge   ....

strange   dodge   ....

10

3. Unscramble the letters in bold to make a word with the **j** sound.

   There is a **ibrdeg** over the river.  ....

   I forgot to bring my **akjcet**.  ....

   A **engie** came out of the lamp.  ....

4. Can you use the spellings from the box to complete the sentences below?

   | j | ge | dge | g |

   Emma looked in the fri................. for a snack.

   The queen smiled at the ....oyful jester.

   The lar................. dragon chased the knight.

   Tyler had used too much hair ....el.

An Extra Challenge

Prince George and Princess Gina are holding a summer fair. Can you write down all of the things in the picture that contain the **j** sound?

Are your soft g skills legendary? Tick a box.

Silent k, g and w

How It Works

Some words start with a silent letter. You don't say this letter when you read the word out loud.

knew   **g**nash   **w**rite

k and g are silent if they come before **n**.

w is silent if it comes before **r**.

Now Try These

1. Read the words below. If the word contains a silent letter, colour the picture blue. If it doesn't contain a silent letter, colour the picture red.

 keep
 glum
 knight
 wrap

 gnarled
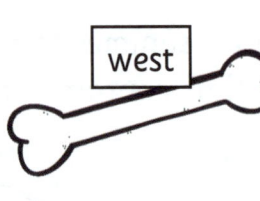 west
 wriggle
 knead

2. Tick the sentence below that uses a silent letter correctly. Can you rewrite the words that are spelt wrong without any mistakes?

I can't find my wruler.   ☐   ....

Ben likes to wrestle.   ☐   ....

Amy has ritten a letter.   ☐

3. Circle the word in bold in each sentence that has the right spelling.

I **know / gnow** the fastest way to the park.

Mimi wants a **knome / gnome** for her garden.

My dog's lead has a **knot / gnot** in it.

Lewis put a **knife / gnife** and fork on the table.

4. Draw lines to join each word to the missing letter, then rewrite the word.

__reck   k   ....

__nit   g   ....

__nat   w   ....

An Extra Challenge

Spike and his friends are talking about a noise they heard.
Can you correct their spelling mistakes to find out what's happening?

There was a nock at the red door.

You're rong! The noise came from the green door.

Be quiet and let me naw this bone!

It was me. I just hit my nee on this vase.

Did you manage to sniff out the silent letters? Tick a box.

Words ending in le, el, al and il

How It Works

The word endings **le**, **el**, **al** and **il** can all sound the same.

jungle   camel   metal   devil

The **le** ending is used most often.

Not many words end in **il**.

Now Try These

1. Draw lines to join each word to the missing letters.

 ev__

 midd__

 lev__

 ped__

 le

 el

 al

 il

2. Circle the right spelling of each word.

capital / capitel

needle / needel

loyel / loyal

puple / pupil

parcal / parcel

tabel / table

16

3. Unscramble the letters in bold to make a word ending in **le**, **el**, **al** or **il**.

The **ilttel** bug walked across a leaf. ➡ ....

Mia got a **pecnli** in the gift shop. ➡ ....

A **patle** fell off the pink flower. ➡ ....

The train went through a **tnuenl**. ➡ ....

4. Can you rewrite these words in the box with the right ending?

arriv__   tow__

bott__

eag__

anim__

nostr__

An Extra Challenge

Erin the Explorer is playing with her friends in the jungle. Can you write down all of the things ending in **le**, **el**, **al** or **il** in the picture?

Did you make it through this word endings jungle? Tick a box.

Words ending in tion and sion

How It Works

Lots of words end in tion or sion.

tion
↓
posi**tion**

sion
↓
divi**sion**

Now Try These

1. Colour in the pictures where the word is spelt correctly. Can you rewrite the words that are spelt wrong in the box without any mistakes?

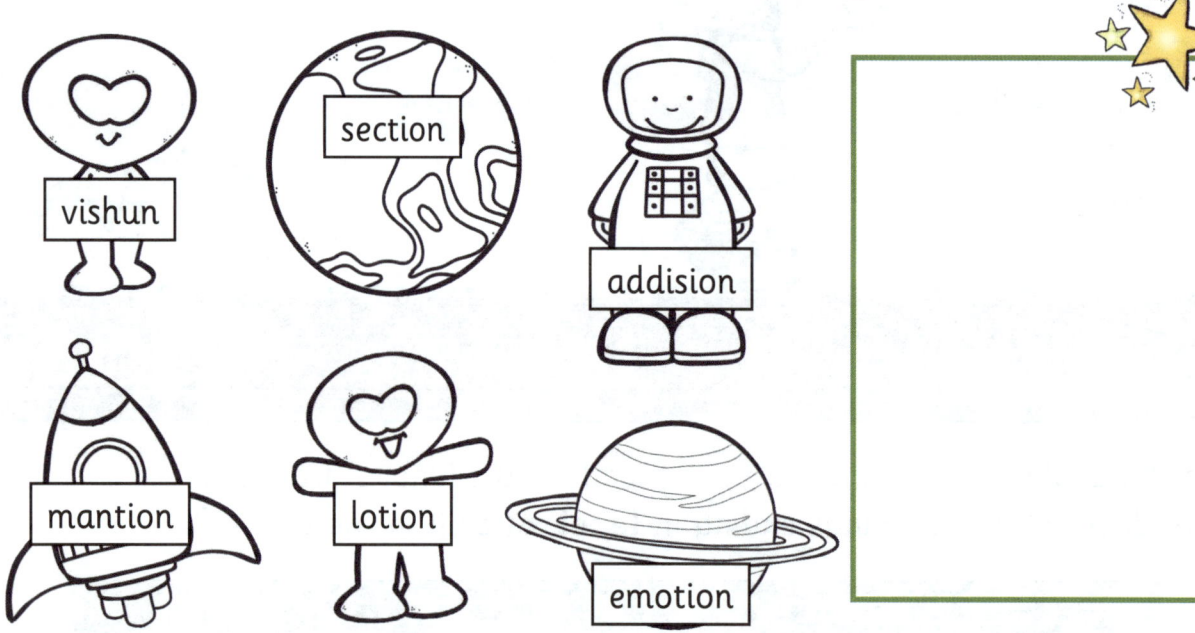

vishun · section · addision · mantion · lotion · emotion

2. Tick the sentences below that are spelt correctly.

We stopped the alien invasion. ☐

Jane likes reading fiction books. ☐

The poster had a big capsion. ☐

3. Circle the right spelling to complete each sentence below.

The doctor gave Sadiq an ………… .   injection   injecsion

There was an ………… in the rocket.   explotion   explosion

Hayley saw a film on the ………… .   televition   television

The witch made a magic ………… .   potion   posion

4. Can you use all the letters on each planet to write a word ending in **tion** or **sion**?

 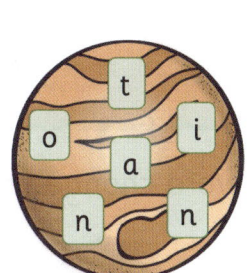  

_ _ _ _ _ _ _ _ _   _ _ _ _ _ _ _ _

_ _ _ _ _ _ _

An Extra Challenge

Ada has written a story about space, but she has made some mistakes. How many can you spot? Can you correct them?

Some aliens were attacking the space stasion. The astronauts had two opshuns. They could either take acsion or fly away. Captain Kim bravely made the decition to speak to the aliens. She knew she had to become friends with them.

Were these pages a blast? Give a box a tick.

Adding ing and ed

How It Works

When you add the suffixes **ing** or **ed** to a word, the root word often stays the same. Sometimes, though, you need to make small changes to the root word.

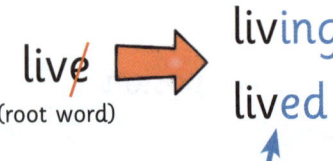 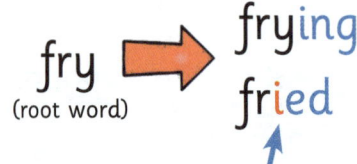 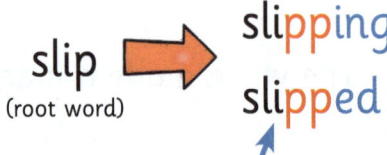

If a word ends in **e**, you remove it before adding ing or ed.

If a word ends in **y**, you might need to change it to an i before adding ed.

If a word ends with a vowel then a consonant, you might need to double the **last letter**.

Now Try These

1. Draw lines to show how each word changes when you add **ed**.

 no spelling change

 double the last letter

2. Circle the word in bold in each sentence that has the right spelling.

The baby is **enjoiing** / **enjoying** the cake.

Kat is **crying** / **crieing** because she fell over.

Asad **carried** / **carryed** a heavy bag.

3. The words below are spelt wrong. Can you rewrite each word with the right spelling?

 bakd

 iceing

 serveed

....

4. Rewrite each word, adding **ing** or **ed** to make a new word.

marry ing    ....

slice ed   ....

swim ing   ....

reply ed    ....

An Extra Challenge

Obasi and his friends are talking about baking. Can you correct their spelling mistakes to find out what's happening?

I'm coverred in batter from makeing a cake.

I'm giveing this cake to my mum.

I tidyed up the kitchen but now it's messy again!

Is adding ing and ed a piece of cake? Put a tick in a box.

Adding er, est and y

How It Works

Adding the suffixes **er**, **est** or **y** to a word is like adding **ing** or **ed**. You might need to remove or change the last letter of the root word.

simpl~~e~~ ➡ simpl**er**   simpl**est**   simpl**y** ← Remove the **e** before you add er, est or y.

nasty ➡ nast**ier**   nast**iest** ← Here, **y** is changed to **i** when you add er or est.

mad ➡ ma**dd**er   ma**dd**est ← Here, the **last letter** of the root word is doubled.

Now Try These

1. Colour in the pictures where the word is spelt correctly.

hoter

larger

jogger

strangeer

2. Tick the sentence below that uses the right spelling of a word ending **y**. Can you rewrite the words that are spelt wrong without any mistakes?

These running shoes smell cheesey. ☐

....

Owen always tells funny jokes. ☐

....

I am wearing red spoty socks. ☐

3. Circle the right spelling of each word.

bigest / biggest   niceest / nicest

rudest / rudeest

messyest / messiest

crispiest / crispyest   saddest / sadest

4. Complete each sentence by adding the ending in the box. You might need to add other letters too.

The fastest run.............. finished in first place.   er

It was the happ.............. day of my life.   est

Kevin is a friendly and chat.............. person.   y

Mo's medal was shin.............. than mine.   er

Friday was the wet.............. day of the week.   est

An Extra Challenge

Use the picture clues to help you spell out the words below. Can you use each word in a sentence?

s _ n _ y   l _ z e _ t   _ i n _ _ r

Did you run rings around these questions? Put a tick in a box.

More suffixes

How It Works

The spelling of most root words doesn't change when you add the suffixes ment, less, ness, ful and ly.

move + ment → movement ← The spelling of the root word stays the same.

Sometimes, the spelling of the root word does change when you add a suffix.

happy + ness → happiness ← The spelling of the word **happy** changes when a suffix is added.

Now Try These

1. Circle the suffix in each row that can be added to the word on the stamp.

   - bright: ment, ness, less
   - power: ful, ly, ness
   - treat: less, ful, ment

2. Rewrite each word below, adding the suffix to make a new word.

   - harm + less → ....
   - short + ly → ....
   - merry + ment → ....

3. Circle the word in bold in each sentence that has the right spelling.

The letter had a **colourrful / colourful** stamp.

I'm **useless / usless** at doing maths homework.

The **heavyness / heaviness** of the parcel made it difficult to carry.

4. Draw lines to join each word to the right suffix, then write out the new word.

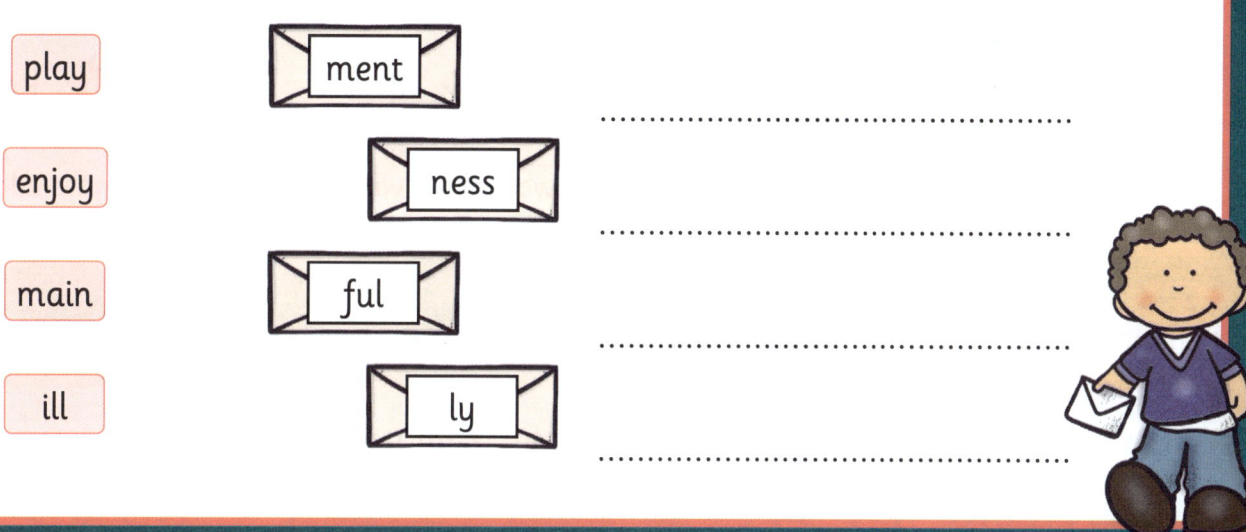

play — ment — ....

enjoy — ness — ....

main — ful — ....

ill — ly — ....

An Extra Challenge

Fill in the gaps in these words that end with a suffix.
Then find the words in the wordsearch. Use the pictures to help you.

 l __ ve __ y

 p __ ym __ __ t

sa __ ne __ __

 sp __ tl __ __ s

```
H A N D F U L S
R D V E L S F A
A I Q M O X U D
O R U W V E T N
P A Y M E N T E
S P O T L E S S
N E S L Y N E S
```

ha __ df __ l

Did you deliver the answers on these pages? Tick a box.

Adding s and es

How It Works

To make most words into plurals, you add **s** or **es** to the end.

one plan ➡ two plan**s**   one watch ➡ two watch**es**

For words that end with a consonant then **y**, change the **y** to an **i** then add **es**.

sp**y** ➡ sp**ies**   key ➡ key**s**

If a word ends with a **vowel** then **y**, just add **s**.

Now Try These

1. Circle the plurals that are spelt correctly. Can you rewrite the plurals that are spelt wrong in the box without any mistakes?

ponies

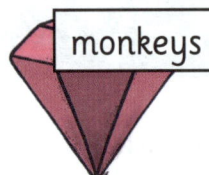
monkeys

houses

chimnies

speechs

babys

ashes

floweres

2. As well as plurals, some verbs end in **s** and **es**. Tick the sentences below where the verb in bold is spelt correctly.

A good spy **tries** to stay hidden at all times. ☐

Rosie **hurrys** to catch the train every morning. ☐

Dad **says** that we can go bowling on Friday. ☐

Leo **studys** often for his secret agent exam. ☐

3. Can you add the right ending to each word to make it into a plural?

body ....

enemy ....

lady ....

An Extra Challenge

Using plurals, can you describe something in the picture below? Write down as many sentences as you can.

Mission accomplished? Tick a box to show how you did.

27

Tricky words

How It Works

Some words are tricky to spell because they don't follow normal spelling rules.

w**a**ter

Some words contain sounds that aren't spelt as you might think. In 'water', the **or** sound is spelt **a**.

clim**b**

Other words contain silent letters that you might not expect, like the silent **b** at the end of 'climb'.

Now Try These

1. Colour in the pictures where the word is spelt correctly.

fathur | move | parth | cold | child

2. Circle the word in bold in each sentence with the right spelling.

My **parents** / **pairents** took us all camping.

There is lots of **sugar** / **shugar** in chocolate.

I spilled my tea all over the **flore** / **floor** .

We sailed around the **hoal** / **whole** lake.

The sunset is really **pretty** / **pritty** tonight.

3. The words below are spelt wrong.
   Can you rewrite them without any mistakes?

   peepel   dore   cloeths

   ....

4. Tick the phrases below where the word in bold is spelt correctly.
   Can you rewrite the other phrases in the box without any mistakes?

   a **bewtiful** view ☐

   the **busy** street ☐

   a bag of **munee** ☐

   the **wild** animal ☐

An Extra Challenge

Can you use the clues to fill in the crossword below?
The first one has been done for you.

Across:
1. ~~to smash~~
3. to get better
5. to grasp
6. not rich
7. certain

Down:
2. friendly
4. each
5. 60 minutes

1 across: b r e a k
3 across: _ m _ r _ _
5 across: _ l d
6 across: _ o _
7 across: u _

Are you con-tent with how these pages went? Put a tick in a box.

Answers

Pages 2-3 — Words ending in y
1. Blue: berry, rely, baby, shy / Red: chimney, trolley
2. 'The train went through the valley.', 'I saw hot-air balloons in the sky.'
3. You should have circled: happy, penny, hockey, party
4. dry, fry, apply, reply

   An Extra Challenge
   journey, fly, ferry

Pages 4-5 — Short vowel sounds
1. squad, swamp, wand, stop
2. huney (honey), muther (mother)
3. done, glove, oven, money
4. watch, squabbles, waddled, squashed

   An Extra Challenge
   The mistakes are: munth (month), quontity (quantity), wosps (wasps), squot (squat), anuther (another)

Pages 6-7 — or and ur
1. You should have circled: arlways, swalm, horl
2. word, worst, worship
3. homework, warmth, worse, world, wardrobe
4. You should have circled: all, reward, almost, warden

   An Extra Challenge
   Any sentences that use words containing the or or ur sound, e.g. A warm man is getting an award.

Pages 8-9 — Soft c
1. nicer, fence, spicy
2. race, fancy, decided
3. You should have circled: since, pace, signs, voice
4. 'a nice polar bear', 'the singing reindeer'
   You should have written: a helpful recipe, outside the bank

   An Extra Challenge
   You should have found: frost, juicy, mice, circus

Pages 10-11 — Soft g
1. object, joke, giant, gentle, jewel, engine
2. ege (edge), chandge (change)
3. bridge, jacket, genie
4. fridge, joyful, large, gel

   An Extra Challenge
   Any words with a j sound, e.g. orange, pigeon, sausage, jumper

Pages 12-13 — Silent k, g and w
1. Blue: knight, wrap, gnarled, wriggle, knead / Red: keep, glum, west
2. 'Ben likes to wrestle.'
   You should have written: ruler, written
3. You should have circled: know, gnome, knot, knife
4. wreck, knit, gnat

   An Extra Challenge
   The mistakes are: nock (knock), rong (wrong), naw (gnaw), nee (knee)

Pages 14-15 — Wild West round-up
You should have circled:
bruther
choise
tenshun
becose
traval
nelt
smileing
taxs

Crossword — Across: brother, choice, smiling, tension
Down: travel, axe, smile, trust, knelt

Pages 16-17 — Words ending in le, el, al and il
1. evil, middle, level, pedal
2. You should have circled: capital, needle, loyal, parcel, pupil, table
3. little, pencil, petal, tunnel
4. arrival, towel, bottle, eagle, animal, nostril

   An Extra Challenge
   Any words ending le, el, al or il, e.g. fossil, trowel, animal, castle

Pages 18-19 — Words ending in tion and sion
1. You should have coloured: section, lotion, emotion
   You should have written: vision, addition, mansion
2. 'We stopped the alien invasion.', 'Jane likes reading fiction books.'
3. You should have circled: injection, explosion, television, potion
4. version, nation, mention

   An Extra Challenge
   The mistakes are: stasion (station), opshuns (options), acsion (action), decition (decision)

Pages 20-21 — Adding ing and ed
1. no spelling change: help, cook, play
   double the last letter: chop, chat, skip
2. You should have circled: enjoying, crying, carried
3. baked, icing, served
4. marrying, sliced, swimming, replied

   An Extra Challenge
   The mistakes are: coverred (covered), makeing (making), giveing (giving), tidyed (tidied)

Pages 22-23 — Adding er, est and y
1. You should have coloured: larger, jogger
2. 'Owen always tells funny jokes.'
   You should have written: cheesy, spotty
3. You should have circled: biggest, nicest, rudest, messiest, crispiest, saddest
4. You should have written: runner, happiest, chatty, shinier, wettest

   An Extra Challenge
   sunny, laziest, winner
   Any sentences, e.g. It was sunny, so I went for a run.

Pages 24-25 — More suffixes
1. brightness, powerful, treatment
2. harmless, shortly, merriment
3. You should have circled: colourful, useless, heaviness
4. playful, enjoyment, mainly, illness

   An Extra Challenge
   You should have found: lovely, sadness, payment, spotless, handful

Pages 26-27 — Adding s and es
1. You should have circled: ponies, monkeys, houses, ashes
   You should have written: chimneys, speeches, babies, flowers
2. 'A good spy tries to stay hidden at all times.', 'Dad says that we can go bowling on Friday.'
3. bodies, enemies, ladies

   An Extra Challenge
   Any sentences that use plurals, e.g. The jellies are on the tables.

Pages 28-29 — Tricky words
1. You should have coloured: move, cold, child
2. You should have circled: parents, sugar, floor, whole, pretty
3. people, door, clothes
4. 'the busy street', 'the wild animal'
   You should have written: a beautiful view, a bag of money

   An Extra Challenge
   Across: 3. improve, 5. hold, 6. poor, 7. sure
   Down: 2. kind, 4. every, 5. hour